MW01204549

MILLARD FILLMORE

The Presidents of the United States

George Washington
1789–1797

John Adams
1797–1801

Thomas Jefferson
1801–1809

James Madison
1809–1817

James Monroe
1817–1825

John Quincy Adams
1825–1829

Andrew Jackson
1829–1837

Martin Van Buren
1837–1841

William Henry Harrison
1841

John Tyler
1841–1845

James Polk
1845–1849

Zachary Taylor
1849–1850

Millard Fillmore
1850–1853

Franklin Pierce
1853–1857

James Buchanan
1857–1861

Abraham Lincoln
1861–1865

Andrew Johnson
1865–1869

Ulysses S. Grant
1869–1877

Rutherford B. Hayes
1877–1881

James Garfield
1881

Chester Arthur
1881–1885

Grover Cleveland
1885–1889

Benjamin Harrison
1889–1893

Grover Cleveland
1893–1897

William McKinley
1897–1901

Theodore Roosevelt
1901–1909

William H. Taft
1909–1913

Woodrow Wilson
1913–1921

Warren Harding
1921–1923

Calvin Coolidge
1923–1929

Herbert Hoover
1929–1933

Franklin D. Roosevelt
1933–1945

Harry Truman
1945–1953

Dwight Eisenhower
1953–1961

John F. Kennedy
1961–1963

Lyndon Johnson
1963–1969

Richard Nixon
1969–1974

Gerald Ford
1974–1977

Jimmy Carter
1977–1981

Ronald Reagan
1981–1989

George H. W. Bush
1989–1993

William J. Clinton
1993–2001

George W. Bush
2001–present

MILLARD FILLMORE

TED GOTTFRIED

mc **Marshall Cavendish**
Benchmark
New York

For Harriet

Acknowledgments
I am grateful to personnel of the New York Central Research Library, the Mid-Manhattan Library, the Queensboro Public Library, the New York State Historical Society, and many others for their aid in gathering material for this book. Also, gratitude is due George Fried for providing historical material not otherwise easily come by. Finally, thanks and much love to my wife, Harriet Gottfried, who—as always—read and critiqued the manuscript. Her help was invaluable, but any shortcomings in the work are mine alone.
—Ted Gottfried

Marshall Cavendish Benchmark
99 White Plains Road
Tarrytown, NY 10591-9001
www.marshallcavendish.us

Library of Congress Cataloging-in-Publication Data

Gottfried, Ted.
Millard Fillmore / by Ted Gottfried.
p. cm. — (Presidents and Their Times)
Summary: "This series provides comprehensive information on the presidents of the United States and places each within his historical and cultural context. It also explores the formative events of his times and how he responds"—Provided by publisher.
Includes bibliographical references and index.
ISBN-13: 978-0-7614-2431-4
1. Fillmore, Millard, 1800-1874—Juvenile literature. 2. Presidents—United States—Biography—Juvenile literature. 3. United States—Politics and government—1849-1853—Juvenile literature. I. Title. II. Series.
E427.G67 2007
973.6'4092—dc22
[B]2006019707

Editor: Christine Florie
Publisher: Michelle Bisson
Art Director: Anahid Hamparian
Series Designer: Alex Ferrari

Photo research by Connie Gardner

Cover photo Millard Fillmore (1800–74) (colour litho), Healy, George Peter Alexander (1808–94) (after)/ Peter Newark American Pictures, Private Collection/The Bridgeman Art Library.

The photographs in this book are used by permission and through the courtesy of: *The Granger Collection:* 3, 6, 8, 11, 17, 21, 22, 26, 28, 34, 39, 40, 49, 56, 57, 58, 61, 68, 69, 71, 77, 79, 80, 83, 85(R). *North Wind Picture Archive:* 10, 51. *Corbis:* 15, 30, 43; Bettmann, 12, 20, 47, 67, 84 (R). *The Bridgeman Art Library:* Little boy reading a book(wic). Hunt, William Henry (1790–1864)/c Chris Beetles, London, U.K. Private Collection, 14, 84(R), 85(L). *Art Resource, NY:* 63.

Printed in Malaysia
1 3 5 6 4 2

CONTENTS

Millard Fillmore was born in January 1800 in a cabin much like this one in upstate New York.

A Child of the Century

*T*he year 1800 marked the beginning of the first full century of the existence of the United States of America. It was a century filled with growth and turmoil and shaped by heroes and villains, and a century in which Americans struggled to be moral and just. Some succeeded, and some failed. The year 1800 also saw the birth of Millard Fillmore, who, in mid-century, would become president of the United States and who, by the end of the century, would be all but obscured by the fog of history.

Fillmore was born on January 7 in a log cabin in Cayuga County, New York, which was then part of the western frontier of the new nation Fillmore would one day lead. He was the second child and the first of five sons of Nathaniel and Phoebe Millard Fillmore. He was named after his mother's family.

Piracy and Bravery

Not much is known about Phoebe Fillmore's family, but records of Nathaniel's go back several generations. Millard Fillmore's great grandfather John was a sailor who once had a violent confrontation with Captain John Phillips, one of the fiercest pirates on the seas. After being captured and kept as slaves by Phillips for nine months, John Fillmore and several other brave crewmates rebelled. They seized weapons, overpowered the pirates, and finally sailed back to Boston Harbor. There, a maritime court gave John Fillmore Captain Phillip's silver-hilted sword in honor of his defeating one of the sea's most wicked pirates.

PIRATES, AHOY!

John Fillmore's bravery while on board a pirate ship was a story that was handed down from generation to generation in the Fillmore family. His rebellion on the pirate ship was certainly tense. He was not a violent man by nature, but after suffering cruelty and hardship for three-quarters of a year, he had finally had enough. He had felt the sting of the whip from the boatswain too many times. It had to be stopped.

Quietly, Fillmore and a handful of others waited for a calm night aboard the ship. The crew was drinking and paying little attention to their prisoners. Fillmore confronted the boatswain and immediately ducked as an ax whooshed over the top of his head. He grabbed the weapon. The boatswain's reaction to this was far too slow; seconds later, he was dead. During the fray, four pirates were killed, including Captain John Phillips. Six others were hauled into Boston Harbor and were hanged soon after. All of their gold rings and shoe buckles were given to John Fillmore as rewards for his courage.

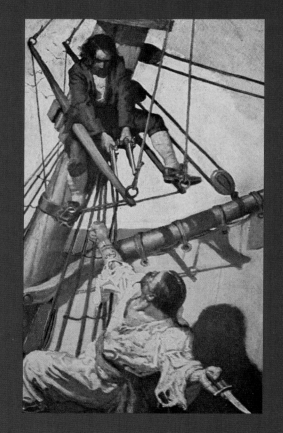

This same sword was later used by John Fillmore's son Nathaniel in both the French and Indian and Revolutionary wars. Over the years it became a prized heirloom in the Fillmore household.

GOD'S ALMIGHTY GENTLEMAN

Nathaniel Fillmore's second son, also named Nathaniel, was Millard Fillmore's father. Although organized religion played no role in his household, he was known to his contemporaries as one of "God Almighty's gentlemen," and there was always a King James Bible in their home during Millard's childhood. Nathaniel's one creed was "Do right!" and he made every effort to pass it on to his children.

Fillmore's mother, Phoebe, was remembered by him as a gentle woman who, despite suffering from an undiagnosed but lingering illness, had a sunny disposition. She needed it, for misfortune struck the family not long after Fillmore's birth. They lost their home and the land on which it stood and moved to the Finger Lakes region of upstate New York.

THE HOMESTEADERS

The Fillmore homestead was part of almost two million acres of New York land known as the Military Tract. It had originally been set aside for veterans of the Revolutionary War. Millard Fillmore's grandfather had fought in the war, but his father had not. An official team of commissioners found that his title to the land on which the family had settled was illegal. The Fillmores packed up their belongings again and moved north to an area then known as Sempronius, sometimes referred to as Locke (later the Finger Lakes). There, Nathaniel Fillmore and a younger brother leased a

130-acre farm. They were **tenant farmers**, otherwise known as sharecroppers. They did all the hard, physical work on the land, while the landowner provided the animals, tools, seed, and equipment. In return, tenant farmers were given a small share of the money made from the sale of the crops.

Young Millard Fillmore grew up on this farm. He was assigned chores even as a toddler. As he grew older, he took on more and more work. Much of it was labor that required a bent back and strong arms—hoeing corn, mowing hay with the curved blade of a

As tenant farmers, the Fillmores worked the land and were repaid with a small portion of the sale of the crops they had grown.

scythe, and reaping wheat. In springtime Millard prepared the soil for planting with a wooden plow that was pulled by a mule, when one was handy. When a mule was nowhere to be found, Millard plowed the soil himself. In winter he chopped wood for the fireplace.

When Millard did not feel like working, he would steal away to hunt rabbits with his father's rifle or settle under a tree on the banks of Skaneateles Lake, cast a line for fish, and

Young Millard was responsible for certain chores on the farm, such as harvesting wheat.

doze. His father considered such activities lazy and evil. "No man," he lectured Millard, "ever prospered from wasting his time in sporting." These were pursuits, Nathaniel told his son, suited only to "uncivilized Indians." His father's attitude toward Native Americans was one of Millard's earliest contacts with the bigotry that would continue to appear in his later life.

A Lesson in Tyranny

Nathaniel Fillmore found farming a harsh and unrewarding way of life. With a growing family, he had no choice but to be a farmer. He and Phoebe decided that their eldest son, Millard, should have other options. Hard work had made Millard a sturdy youth. When he was fifteen years old, he was apprenticed to learn the business of carding wool and dressing cloth. The job involved separating fibers of raw wool to spin into yarn and treating woven materials

At fifteen, Millard left the farm to apprentice for a cruel employer in the wool and cloth business.

with gum or starch to stiffen them in order to make garments or other items. The work was painstakingly tedious and boring.

It was an unhappy apprenticeship for Millard. The workshop was located more than a hundred miles from his home. His employer was an impatient and demanding man with a brutal streak, who threatened to strike Millard when his fingers were not nimble enough. In retaliation Millard picked up a small ax and threatened his employer. Three months later Millard borrowed $30 and paid off his obligation to the cloth maker. Now free, he walked one hundred miles back to his family.

Years later Fillmore described the incident in his autobiography. He concluded that "this injustice which was no more than other apprentices have suffered and will suffer had a marked effect on my character. It made me feel for the weak and unprotected, and to hate the insolent tyrant in every station of life."

READING AND LEARNING

Still determined that his eldest son should not have to suffer the hardships and disappointments of farm life as he did, Millard's father again arranged for Millard to be apprenticed to a cloth-processing establishment near the village of New Hope. Once more, living far from home, it was a lonely life for a young boy who was fifteen years old. It was then that his real education began, as he started to steal and borrow books.

As a child, Millard had been taught how to read, but aside from his family's King James Bible, he had little opportunity to do so. He knew virtually nothing about grammar or how to phrase things correctly—skills that he would need desperately in his future life in politics. Now in his teens and determined to improve himself, he bought a small dictionary and began memorizing words to enlarge his vocabulary. Sometimes he would secretly glance at the book while carding wool and silently work out the pronunciation of words to himself.

When he was seventeen years old, Millard heard about a small library that offered to loan books to the public. He joined and soon was reading eagerly. Eventually, he found himself drawn to books dealing with history, government, and law.

Roughly two years later a private academy was established in New Hope. Recognizing the need to improve his education, Millard enrolled while still apprenticing at the cloth-processing establishment. The school was coeducational, and for the first time, Millard came into close social contact with females other than his sisters. One of them was Abigail Powers, who would one day become his wife.

FALLING IN LOVE

Two years older than her future husband, Abigail had many of the social graces that Millard still lacked. The daughter of Reverend Lemuel Powers and the sister of a judge, she was a poised, well-educated, and confident young woman with an easy manner that hid her pious nature. By contrast, at this stage in his life, the nineteen-year-old Millard must have seemed a bumbling backwoods

To broaden his vocabulary and reading skills, Millard studied the dictionary.

lad, ill suited to the social norms followed by the Powers family. Nevertheless, Abigail was drawn to him. She was tolerant of his clumsiness and poor manners, accepting of the gaps in his education, and attracted to his earnest manner and muscular appearance.

As for Millard, he was smitten from the first. Abigail's long, black hair, large, dark eyes, and slender frame all attracted him. However, it was the strength of her features, enhanced by the steadfastness of her gaze as she listened to him spin out his hopes, ambitions, and dreams that claimed his love. At this point in their lives, Abigail was more adept in the art of conversation than Millard was, but she was also

Abigail Powers married Millard Fillmore in 1826.

a good listener. Besides, she was genuinely interested in his plans and was already aware that their futures might well be intertwined. Her gentleness may have reminded Millard of his mother, but unlike that good woman, Abigail was not a passive person.

Throughout the year of 1819, Millard and Abigail saw a lot of each other. What began as a friendship deepened into a courtship and then into love. Marriage, however, was not yet a possibility. Millard was determined to establish himself career-wise before marrying, and Abigail respected his decision.

The Pettifog Incident

Around this time Millard's father, unable to survive financially on the farm at Sempronius, was forced to give it up. He moved his family to Montville, where he once again became a tenant farmer. This time his landlord was the county judge Walter Wood. Aware of his son's feeling that there was little future in the carding workshop and of Millard's ambition to advance himself, Nathaniel persuaded the judge to give Millard a two-month trial as a clerk in his law office. At the end of Millard's trial period, Judge Wood, a Quaker, told Millard, "If thee has an ambition for distinction, and can sacrifice everything else to success, the law is the road that leads to honors; and if thee can get rid of thy engagement to serve as an apprentice, I would advise thee to come back again and study law."

The judge offered to advance Millard $65 while he studied, with the understanding that it would be paid back once the young man actually began to practice law. In addition, Millard secured a three-month position teaching elementary school to help with his living expenses. At the end of the three months, Millard returned to Judge Wood's office and settled down to a combination of clerking duties and the study of law.

Less than two years after they began to work together, Judge Wood and Millard had a disagreement. Without letting the judge know it, Millard had been taking small cases to court and keeping the fees for himself. These cases were minor ones, and prosecuting them was often referred to as pettifogging, or making a big deal out of a minor legal issue. Millard told Judge Wood he had done it simply because he needed the money, but the judge was still angry. He told Millard that he had to stop doing it immediately or leave the practice.

It was a hard decision for Millard, but finally, he chose to leave. He was worried that Judge Wood was more concerned with keeping him dependent than with helping him to become a lawyer. When he left, he gave the judge an IOU for the $65 Wood had advanced him. He later paid it back with interest.

SUCCESS AND MARRIAGE

At first Millard Fillmore took another teaching assignment, this time in the growing city of Buffalo.

As a young man, Fillmore was given the opportunity to study law and clerk for Judge Walter Wood.

Then, he got a job clerking in a Buffalo law firm. He continued studying law over the next few years and in 1823 was admitted to the New York State bar. Rather than compete with the many lawyers in Buffalo, however, Fillmore opened his first law office in the village of East Aurora.

There, his law practice consisted mostly of dealing with mortgages, writing wills, settling land title disputes, and collecting debts. Nevertheless, he established himself in the community and forged his first political connections by taking an active role in community affairs, including the development of transportation.

As a result, he was appointed commissioner of deeds for the region. It was a modestly lucrative post, and his fees for recording deeds increased his income.

By 1826 Millard Fillmore was a well-regarded and successful young, small-town lawyer. By then Abigail had been patiently waiting seven years for their wedding to take place. On February 5, 1826, it finally did. The marriage fueled Fillmore's ambition even more, and Abigail's faith in him gave him the confidence to further his career. That same year the Fillmores left East Aurora and moved to Buffalo. It would prove to be Millard Fillmore's first step into the world of big-time politics.

DRAWN TO POLITICS *Two*

*T*he Free and Accepted Masons, also known as **Freemasons**, are one of the largest secret fraternal (all-male) orders in the world. The first U.S. president, George Washington, was a Mason. So were many of the nation's Founding Fathers, including Paul Revere, John Hancock, John Paul Jones, and Benjamin Franklin. Masons' signatures can be found on both the Declaration of Independence and the Constitution.

Similar in many ways to the Elks, Shriners, Lions, and Kiwanis, the Masons have strict requirements for acceptance into their organization. Their basic tenets are brotherly love (tolerance and respect toward others), relief (helping the community through charitable, or philanthropic, activities), and truth (high morals). Because they also have secret, or private, oaths and practices, the Masons often were the target of suspicion and prejudice. Sometimes they were even attacked politically, particularly during the 1820s and '30s. Concerned that the Masons might be able to greatly influence the government, the **Anti-Masonic Party** was formed. Millard Fillmore, a young man who was just getting his feet wet in the world of politics, was inspired by the many editorials written against the Masons in the *Anti-Masonic Enquirer*, a local newspaper edited by a man named Thurlow Weed. It was this anti-Masonic attitude on which Fillmore chose to base his early political career.

THE ANTI-MASONIC MOVEMENT

As he prospered, Fillmore hired a student clerk named Nathan Kelsey Hall to work in his law office. This arrangement worked

A New Man

By the time he went to Buffalo, Millard Fillmore was no longer the awkward backwoods lad of his youth. With Abigail's help, he had learned to watch his grammar and modulate his speech, to listen carefully, and to study the person speaking rather than just listening to the words spoken. His manners had been honed, and he had developed an attitude that was both respectful of others and serious. Although he did not always express himself well, he was listened to respectfully. He chose his words carefully, and his conclusions were well thought out.

Fillmore could afford clothes suitable for a lawyer by that time, and he dressed meticulously. Following the fashion of the respectable men he dealt with, Fillmore carried a silver-knobbed walking stick. His face took on a prosperous roundness, an emblem of respectability.

out so well that Fillmore eventually took on Hall as a partner. The firm of Fillmore and Hall was successful and became well-known and admired throughout the state. As time passed, like many lawyers, Fillmore found himself attracted to politics. The Anti-Masonic Movement was sweeping over western New York, and Fillmore was drawn to it.

Anti-Masonic attitudes began to grow, fueled primarily by a rumor spread in 1826 about the murder of a man named William Morgan. According to gossip, Morgan was initially arrested for stealing and was jailed for his crime. Not long after, a group of unidentified people kidnapped him from his cell and killed him. A number of people believed that the kidnappers

William Morgan was allegedly abducted by Masons who believed he was planning to publish a book on secret Masonic rituals.

were Masons who suspected that Morgan was going to reveal their secrets in a book, and that he was killed in order to prevent that from happening. In response, anger against the Masons began to grow, and newspapers and church leaders condemned the Masons as murderers. The Masons' refusal to cooperate with the investigation that followed did not improve the situation. Many Masonic chapters folded, and members walked away from the organization.

POLITICAL BOSS THURLOW WEED

Like Fillmore, Thurlow Weed had been born in the wilderness—in his case, in the Catskill Mountains—and had dedicated himself to becoming an influential newspaper editor. Soon, he was using his journalistic abilities to promote his own political career. He won a seat in the New York State Assembly, where his skill at back-room politicking and deal making raised him to a leadership position. In 1824 he successfully manipulated his fellow legislators into giving New York's presidential electoral vote to John Quincy Adams. When, however, Adams's popularity waned and Andrew Jackson seemed clearly destined to overcome his upcoming 1828 reelection campaign, the influence of Thurlow Weed declined. To regain it, Weed needed a winning issue that would collect votes and

Thurlow Weed formed the Anti-Masonic Party in order to rekindle his declining popularity in New York politics.

that he could turn into political capital. The Anti-Masonic movement was that issue. Weed successfully channeled the movement into the Anti-Masonic Party, founded in 1828.

In July and then again in August 1828, Millard Fillmore attended New York State Anti-Masonic Party meetings, which, to a large extent, had been organized by Thurlow Weed. The Weed scheme was to wait and rally the Anti-Masons at the last minute to throw their voting power behind President Adams and against the Democratic challenger, Jackson, who was himself a Mason. Weed did not foresee that fanatics would seize control of the Anti-Masonic Party and demand an independent ticket that would get enough support to cost Adams the New York State vote and the election.

By the time of the election Fillmore had become a committed follower of Thurlow Weed. Weed knew Fillmore's reputation as a committed Anti-Mason and so chose him as a candidate for the New York State Legislature. As a result, Fillmore was one of fifteen candidates elected to that body under the banner of the Anti-Masonic Party. Weed was quick to mend his fences with the Anti-Masonic radicals, and under his guidance, the fifteen legislators influenced much of the legislation that was considered. Weed proposed many of the legislative ideas, but it was Fillmore— soft-spoken, courteous, and impressive—who pushed through his programs. These included granting state charters for turnpike companies that collected tolls, as well as for ferries and banks. Weed worked hand-in-glove with the businessmen who profited from these enterprises, and in the legislature, it was said, Fillmore greased the wheels for them. Altogether, Fillmore served three highly successful terms in the legislature.

Millard Fillmore became a father for the first time in 1828 when his son, Millard Powers Fillmore, was born. Four years later

Abigail gave birth to a baby girl, Mary Abigail Fillmore. The Fillmores were prominent and accepted members of Buffalo society. The backwoods bumpkin was a creature of the past. The earnest, soft-spoken lawyer, family man, and legislator had arrived in the person of Millard Fillmore.

EMBRACING UNITARIANISM

Organized religion had played no part in Fillmore's upbringing, and although Abigail had been the daughter of a minister, she had not introduced churchgoing into the early years of their marriage. Now, whether for the sake of the children, for reasons of social acceptance, or to enhance Fillmore's credentials for higher office, in 1831 the Fillmores decided to join a church.

They chose one of the most tolerant denominations available to them, the Unitarian church. Unitarianism focuses on religious tolerance, encouraging members to think through matters of morality and spirituality for themselves. This self-reliance, rather than obedience to doctrine, had great appeal to Fillmore, who was, above all else, a practical man.

Millard and Abigail Fillmore remained Unitarians throughout their lives, even though some of the church's tenets went against many of the policies Fillmore embraced as a politician. Not only would he be attacked by Unitarian ministers such as Theodore Parker, but the Fillmores' own Unitarian pastor "displayed an implacable hatred for Fillmore's policies."

THE WASHINGTON SCENE

With the backing of Thurlow Weed, Fillmore was elected to the New York State House of Representatives in 1828. He continued to practice law, building his solid reputation with the people of his community. He was extremely popular in his county, and it came as little surprise when he was elected to the U.S. House of Representatives in 1832. He was one of a number of Anti-Masonic Party candidates. Nevertheless, Fillmore soon realized that the party itself was fragmenting and losing popular support,

Supporting Religious Tolerance

Although the basic practice of Unitarianism can be found throughout history, it was not until the late 1700s that the first organized Unitarian church appeared in the United States. Considered heretics then and even today, Unitarians believe in religious tolerance above all else. They firmly support the right of individuals to develop their own unique religious opinions. Unitarians place their faith in a God who is gentle and kind, not one who condemns sinners to eternal damnation in hell. Instead of believing in the Holy Trinity of the Father, Son, and the Holy Spirit, Unitarians see God as a singular entity that embraces and welcomes everyone into heaven. They also believe that Jesus Christ was a human religious leader rather than a deity. He was to be followed rather than worshipped.

Unitarians historically have been involved with all aspects of social and political change, such as supporting the abolition of slavery and the right of women to vote. Many congregations included freed slaves and were led by female ministers at a time when this simply was not done. Along with Fillmore, five other presidents have belonged to the Unitarian church: John Adams, Thomas Jefferson, James Madison, John Quincy Adams, and William Howard Taft.

and that its Anti-Masonic principles were becoming more and more irrelevant to the business of government in Washington. Cautiously, Fillmore began seeking new alliances.

He had the good fortune to make a favorable impression on one of the most important national personalities in Washington, Senator Daniel Webster of Massachusetts. A leader of the National Republican wing of the Jeffersonian Republican Party, which had run John Quincy Adams for president, Webster was soon to be one of the founders of the **Whig Party**, which would

absorb large numbers of Anti-Masons, including Fillmore. The paternal interest that Webster took in Fillmore resulted in the young lawyer's being admitted to practice before the U.S. Supreme Court.

Through Webster, Fillmore met Supreme Court justice John McLean. With an arrogance that was unusual for a congressman new to Washington, Fillmore decided that McLean would be an ideal candidate for president in the 1836 election, which was still three years away. Fillmore worked to forge alliances to support McLean's candidacy, but the idea fizzled out long before the election. However, it did focus attention on Fillmore as a person carving out a role for himself in national politics.

Senator Daniel Webster took a liking to Fillmore, and helped him gain the opportunity to practice law before the U.S. Supreme Court.

THE WHIG PARTY

The Whig Party formed during the mid-1830s. It was made up of people who did not like President Andrew Jackson for one reason or another. The abolitionists were angry with Jackson for owning slaves and expanding slavery into the new U.S. territories. Businessmen were unhappy with his apparent lack of support for banks, and farmers were disappointed with his failure to support land improvements, such as building canals and turnpikes.

With a passionate belief in a strong government, the Whigs wanted a president who would not only look out for the economy, but also mandate morality. They felt that ideals such as temperance (abstaining from alcohol), public education, church attendance, and for some, freedom from slavery, should be required. By 1848 the party began to lose prominence, and its members eventually switched to the Republican Party.

THE BANKING CRISIS

In 1837 the United States was plunged into a financial panic. President Jackson's supporters controlled the House of Representatives. They blamed the head of the Bank of the United States, Nicholas Biddle, for the turmoil sweeping the nation. Anti-Jackson representatives such as Fillmore blamed the president. In the Senate, Daniel Webster led the attack against President Jackson.

Jackson did not approve of the Second Bank of the United States because of rumors of fraud and corruption. Therefore, he placed millions of dollars in federal tax revenue into other private

A political cartoon deals with the unemployment, lack of shipping, and hard times of the Panic of 1837. The glasses and white hat symbolize Andrew Jackson, believed to be the reason for the misery of the times.

banks. This hit the Second Bank very hard, as it relied on the government's deposits. The bank began losing money, and in desperation, Biddle demanded payment on all outstanding loans and stopped granting any new ones. Needless to say, clients were shocked and angry. Finally, they pressured Biddle to reinstate his previous loan policies. There was very little money to go around, and when the bank's charter expired in 1836, it was turned into a normal bank. Five years later it went bankrupt.

Fillmore regarded the anti-Biddle campaign as antibusiness and destructive to banking practices in his home state. He was silent on the issue until April 17, 1834, when he made a speech asserting that Jackson's policies were responsible for the depressed state of business, that the income of the general population had fallen by 25 percent, and that the people "were suffering by the act of the government."

FILLMORE VERSUS VAN BUREN

The freshman congressman Millard Fillmore came up for reelection in 1834. At this time Fillmore was urging what was left of the Anti-Masonic Party to disband and support the Whigs. They refused, and instead insisted that Fillmore run for reelection on the Anti-Masonic ticket. Fillmore turned them down. Believing that the Whig Party was not yet strong enough in his district to elect a congressman, he decided not to run for reelection at all.

Two years later, Fillmore ran for Congress as a Whig and won, but the Whigs did not capture the presidency. The Democrat Martin Van Buren was elected to that office. Fillmore became his most determined opponent in Congress.

The issue between them was the system of **free banking**, which Fillmore supported. This called for banks to operate as independent businesses, free of interference or control by the federal government. It was a system, Fillmore believed, under which industry and commerce would flourish. President Van Buren, on the other hand, was influenced by the financial depression from which the nation was just emerging. He feared that without federal regulations, banks would overinvest, extending themselves until some would inevitably fail. Depositors would lose their savings, and the people would fall victim to yet another depression. He wanted to "divorce" government from the banking sector and create an independent treasury.

President Van Buren (right) and Millard Fillmore clashed over the issue of free banking.

Throughout this term and his reelection in 1838, Fillmore locked horns with Van Buren over the question of free banking. Meanwhile, the Whig Party was growing, winning political contests in many parts of the country in the 1838 election. The Whigs won enough seats in the House of Representatives to worry the Democratic Party.

A QUESTION OF SEATING

The dispute was heated. On the face of it, the Democrats had won control of the House in the 1838 election. When five newly elected New Jersey Whig congressmen presented to the Congress certificates of election signed by New Jersey's Whig governor, the five Democrats they had defeated claimed that fraud and violence had cheated them of their rightful places in the House. The five contested seats would determine whether Democrats retained control of the House or whether Whigs captured the majority.

Not counting the five disputed seats, the Democrats were in nominal control of the proceedings. They refused to let the New Jersey Whigs take their seats until the House was organized. "Organized" meant setting up the committees and choosing the heads of those committees for the period until the next election. One of these committees would be the Election Committee, which would decide the question of who should be seated as the duly elected representatives of New Jersey.

After much argument a compromise was reached. A committee was appointed to study the evidence. Millard Fillmore was a minority Whig member of it. The five Whigs and five Democrats who contested the seats were sent back to New Jersey to get evidence to support their claims. It was a ridiculous situation. No sooner had the ten returned than the Democratic leadership waved aside the evidence and seated the five New Jersey Democrats.

Fillmore was outraged. When he attempted to argue the decision, however, the Democratic speaker of the house silenced him. Finally, Fillmore did speak, and he spoke passionately in words that would echo in the House of Representatives right up to the present: "The majority possesses all the power; the minority have nothing to protect them but the Constitution and the rules of the House," he pointed out, "and if these are broken down, then farewell to freedom, farewell to all that is dear to an American citizen! This hall becomes the temple of despotism, and you, Mr. Speaker, its high-priest." It was a lost cause, but it well may have been Millard Fillmore's finest moment.

POLITICS AND POWER *Three*

$\mathscr{A}$lthough slavery was the most hotly debated issue in the nation during Millard Fillmore's years in Congress, for a long time he tiptoed around it. He proclaimed himself antislavery, but often backed compromises that served to prolong the institution, because he felt that abolitionists were a disruption and distraction for the Whig Party. He was much firmer where other issues were concerned. Chief among them was the question of **tariffs**.

Fillmore had been reelected to what would prove to be his last term in Congress in 1840. He now had seniority, and in 1840 he became chairman of the powerful House Ways and Means Committee. In this position he waged a fierce and ultimately successful battle for the cause of high tariffs.

Tariffs were taxes on goods imported from outside the United States, made in nations where wages were lower. These goods were taxed in order to keep their cost at a high enough level so they would not undercut the price of products made in America. The battle over tariffs was between **free traders** and **protectionists**. Free traders were mostly those who exported goods abroad. They feared, and with good cause, that high tariffs in the United States would provoke high tariffs in other countries, where they sold their products. Most free traders tended to be southerners who exported cotton, hemp, and other agricultural products. Protectionists were mostly northern manufacturers who feared that low-cost foreign goods would cut into their sales. Millard Fillmore, who was both supported by and championed northern business interests, was a leading protectionist.

TARIFFS AND LAND SALES

In 1840 the Whig candidate William Henry Harrison was elected president. Harrison had become a popular hero by defeating an uprising of Shawnee Native Americans at the Battle of Tippecanoe in 1811. The battle gave him his campaign slogan, "Tippecanoe and Tyler too." John Tyler, the Whig vice presidential candidate, was really a Democrat who had challenged the programs of that party's leader, Andrew Jackson. He had been added to the Whig ticket to attract anti-Jackson southern votes. One aspect of his appeal was his free-trade position on tariffs. The protectionist Millard Fillmore would be Tyler's fiercest adversary.

A political cartoon created during the 1840 presidential campaign shows Tyler's hard cider barrel locomotive running down Martin Van Buren's broken-down cab.

Just one month after being sworn in as president during a freezing rain, Harrison contracted pneumonia and died. John Tyler became president, the first vice president in American history to succeed to the office because of a presidential death. One of Tyler's first acts was to veto a Whig-sponsored bill to create a privately owned national bank. Fillmore, who had favored the bill, joined with Daniel Webster in trying to persuade Tyler to sign a compromise bill, but to no avail. Although the Whigs had elected Tyler, Tyler was not going to be a Whig president. He wanted to lower the high tariffs that were in effect when he took office. Fillmore used the power of the House Ways and Means Committee to oppose him. As Fillmore saw it, Tyler was a traitor to the Whig Party. Fillmore devised an ingenious scheme to undermine the president.

At that time the federal government's main sources of income were tariffs and the sale of public lands. Fillmore drew up legislation calling for money from land sales to go directly to the states, rather than to the national treasury. In this way high tariffs would have to be maintained in order for the federal government to pay its bills. Tyler vetoed the legislation. He also vetoed a succession of similar bills, which had either originated in Fillmore's committee or in the Whig-controlled Senate.

The existing high tariffs were due to expire at the end of June 1842. Congressional legislation to extend, reduce, or increase them was required, and it had to be signed by the president, otherwise the tariffs would simply no longer exist. By June the federal government was faced with the serious possibility of not being able to pay its upcoming bills if the matter of income from tariffs were not resolved. Fillmore deliberately set up a roadblock to solving the problem. Since Tyler had vetoed the bills

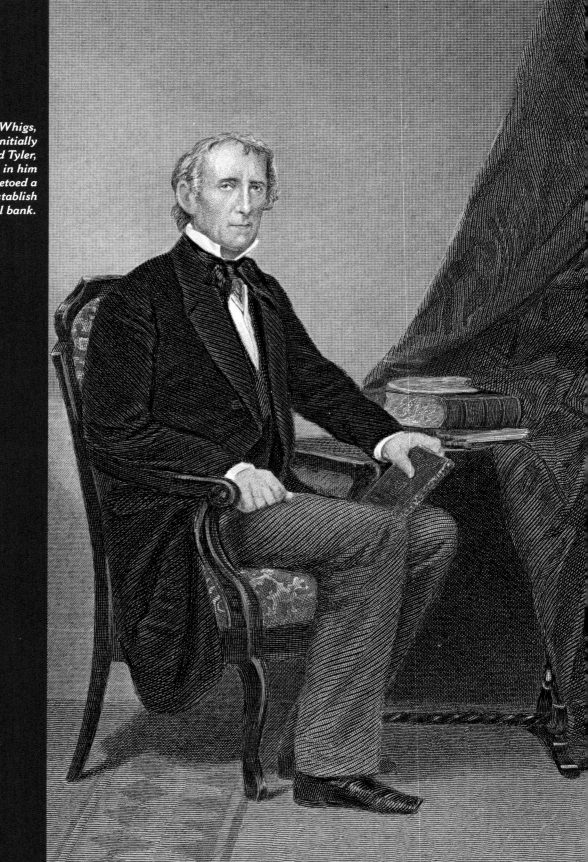

The Whigs, who initially supported Tyler, lost faith in him after he vetoed a bill to establish a national bank.

that Fillmore and the Whigs had offered, he now tied up other bills relating to tariffs and land sales in his Ways and Means Committee, keeping them from going to the floor of the House, where they might be voted on, reconciled with the Senate, and then signed by the president. Then, at the last minute, Fillmore released a bill that allowed the federal government to retain the proceeds from land sales, but increased tariffs by 30 percent. Facing a crisis in government finances, Tyler was forced to sign the bill.

A POLITICAL POLKA

Fillmore's success in raising tariffs earned him national popularity among Whigs. He was a hero to the moneyed men of the North, whose financial support was so key to his success in politics. The acclaim he received fired Fillmore's ambition. He decided not to run for reelection to Congress in 1842, but to bide his time and seek the opportunity to gain higher office.

He had been influenced by an editorial in the Poughkeepsie, New York, journal *Eagle* that called for the Whig Party to nominate him as their vice presidential candidate in 1844. He clipped the item out of the paper and sent it to his longtime political mentor, the Whig Party boss Thurlow Weed. What followed was an intricate political dance.

At first Weed agreed to support Fillmore for vice president. At the same time Weed, in effect the political boss of New York State, was committed to having the Whig Party run his hand-picked candidate, Willis Hall, for governor. Then, however, Hall became ill and was forced to retire from politics. More concerned with retaining his control of New York than about having a relationship with any vice president, Weed now reversed himself and withdrew his support of Fillmore for that office. Instead, he waged an all-out campaign to make Fillmore the Whig candidate for governor. Rather than being flattered by Weed's lavish endorsement of him for governor, Fillmore regarded the withdrawal of Weed's support for his vice presidential candidacy as a betrayal.

Weed's backing was crucial to carrying New York State for the Whigs in a presidential election, and without it, Fillmore's vice presidential candidacy was doomed. He did not want to run for governor, but now Whig national leaders were pressuring him to do so, believing that his presence on the ticket would carry New York State in the presidential election. In the end, as a loyal Whig, Fillmore felt that he had no choice but to run.

SLAVERY AND BIGOTRY

In 1844 the Whig Party was being torn apart by internal factions. Five years earlier abolitionists had formed the nation's first antislavery political organization, the **Liberty Party**, at a national convention in Warsaw, New York, not far from the home of the Fillmore family. Some antislavery northern Whigs defected to the Liberty Party, while others were pressured to push to include Liberty Party abolitionist measures in Whig platform policies. As the pressure grew, Fillmore made it known that he was firmly antislavery while at the same time being careful not to take an activist role in the crusade to end the practice. He was aware that antislavery elements within the Whig Party were not only turning off so-called **cotton Whigs** in the South, who favored Whig trade policies, but also many northern members of the party, who lumped them together with the most fiery abolitionists as hotheads and fanatics. As a candidate for governor Fillmore tried hard not to alienate either the antislavery faction or those who supported the institution.

Another issue pitting Whigs against one another was **nativism**. This policy restricted immigration and curtailed immigrants' rights. It evolved from the pressure caused by the arrival of some 600,000 immigrants—a 5 percent addition to the 1830 U.S. population of roughly 12 million—over the preceding decade. The majority of these immigrants were German and Irish, and most of them were Catholic. To a large extent they settled in the cities of the Northeast. They were poor, often causing friction while competing with other poor people and U.S.-born citizens for jobs, housing, and education.

Whigs battled head to head over nativism as hundreds of thousands of immigrants arrived from Germany and Ireland.

There was also widespread prejudice against Catholics and a fear of influence by the Pope on American politics at the time. In 1843 New York Whigs joined together to form the **American Republican Party** to protect native interests against the aggressiveness of the foreign-born. Other Whigs protested, but nativist elements became more and more influential within the party. In the big cities of New York State, such as New York, Buffalo, and Albany, the Democratic Party capitalized on the Whigs' problem. They recruited foreign-born citizens to their ranks and assisted immigrants in becoming citizens. They then mounted a campaign to convince the new citizens that the Whig Party was anti-immigration and anti-rights for the foreign-born, including those who had become citizens. In particular—and

An anti-Catholic mob in tall hats battle the state militia in 1844 Philadelphia.

with some truth—the Democrats branded the Whigs as the party of anti-Catholicism. A New York Catholic bishop also attacked Whigs for being anti-Catholic.

A BITTER DEFEAT

Privately, Fillmore had reservations about the great number of new immigrants in the nation. In 1832 he had seen a cholera epidemic sweep over Buffalo following a wave of immigration. His firm belief in the separation of church and state also made him suspicious of the Catholic Church. Fearful of the effect of mass immigration on the economy, Fillmore leaned toward restricting it.

He was not, however, a nativist. There were too many foreign-born voters in New York State for Fillmore to join that campaign while running for office. On the contrary, concerned that he would lose the foreign-born vote, he joined with two Buffalo businessmen to found a German-American Whig newspaper in Buffalo. He solicited funds for it from fellow Whigs, pointing out that "it is of great importance both to them and us that the first impressions they receive of our institutions be from a proper source" in their native language.

Fillmore's efforts to secure the votes of the foreign-born were of no avail. Whig candidates suffered a major defeat nationally, losing to the Democrat Silas Wright. In New York State, Whig opinion was divided as to the reason for the loss. Some blamed the antislavery Whigs for burdening the party with abolitionist positions that turned off supporters in the North as well as the South. Others, Fillmore chief among them, blamed the foreign-born, Catholics, and abolitionists for the debacle. Fillmore was bitter about the defeat, and his bitterness would one day result in his becoming a leader of the very nativist groups he had shied away from during his run for governor.

THE MEXICAN WAR

After the election Fillmore reopened a lucrative private law office in Buffalo. He brought his sixteen-year-old son, Powers, into his office as an apprentice. His eleven-year-old daughter, Mary Abigail, was developing into an intense person with a serious interest in music. Fillmore's wife, Abigail, however, was not as energetic as before and suffered intermittently from an undiagnosed illness that sapped her strength. Were it not for Abigail's state of health, Fillmore's life over the next two years would have been completely happy. His practice was thriving, and his popularity was once again growing in the counties of upstate New York.

In April 1846 the United States went to war against Mexico. The conflict put into action President James Polk's policy of **Manifest Destiny**, which envisioned the United States encompassing all of the territory from the Atlantic Ocean to the Pacific Ocean. Writing in the *Buffalo Express* of October 2, 1846, Millard Fillmore expressed Whig opposition to the war. "The interests of the North," he wrote, are being "sacrificed" at a cost of "100 million dollars for the wild and wicked scheme of foreign conquest" to add "another slave territory to the United States." It was Fillmore's strongest public stand against the extension of slavery, and with abolitionist sentiment growing throughout the North, it focused political attention on him once more.

President Polk retaliated mean-spiritedly. Recognizing Fillmore as a Whig spokesperson for the Great Lakes region, he punished the area as a whole, letting it be known that Fillmore was responsible. Shipping on the Great Lakes was increasing at a rapid rate, and improvements were required to keep up with it. Nevertheless, President Polk vetoed a bill passed by Congress to improve the waterways leading into the lakes and to upgrade the docks and anchorages of the ports.

A Stepping-Stone

Politics beckoned Fillmore again in 1847. It was made known to him by mutual Whig friends that if he would run for comptroller of New York State, he would have the support of Boss Weed. Fillmore didn't trust Weed, but at the same time, he recognized

George A. Crofutt's **American Progress** depicts "Manifest Destiny" in white robes, as she floats over the prairie. Below her are signs of Western expansion.

that this might be a stepping-stone to a higher office. As comp-troller his name would be kept before the public. The result was a vindication for Fillmore after his defeat in the governor's race. He was elected state comptroller with the greatest mar-gin over a Democratic opponent—38,000—of any Whig in the history of New York.

MANIFEST DESTINY

The Mexican War was driven by the concept known as Manifest Des-tiny. This belief stated that Americans had a God-given right—in fact, almost a patriotic duty—to expand the country's borders to reach from one sea to the other. It did not matter if anyone else already lived on that land or discovered it first; it was the United States' responsibility to occupy the region in search of income, wealth, and freedom. While this belief was eagerly embraced by most Americans, it was not quite as popular with the nation's neighbors, including the British in Canada, the Mexicans in the southwest, and the Native Americans throughout the area.

This expansion was not always achieved through violence. Often, a great deal of money was offered in exchange for land rights. In both 1835 and 1845 the United States offered to buy California from Mexico for $5 million and then $30 million. Both times, Mexico refused. Emotion between the two countries began to get heated.

Things were further complicated by the Texas war of independence. In the 1820s and '30s Mexico wanted settlers to come to their parts of the country to help develop it. They had two stipulations: the people had to take an oath of allegiance to Mexico and become Catholic, the state religion. Thousands of Americans agreed and moved to the then-Mexican-owned Texas. It was not long, however, before unhappiness began to spread. The Mexicans were frustrated because the Americans began to outnumber them. The Americans did not agree with the Mexican government's decisions, and in 1835 they revolted. Bloody battles followed, and finally, the Mexican president, Antonio López de Santa Anna, while held prisoner, signed two papers known as the Treaties of Velasco. One of the agreements was an open one in which it was stated that "all hostilities would cease and that he would not exercise his influence to cause arms to be taken up against the people of Texas during the present war for independence." The second treaty was a secret one, and it stated that Santa Anna would be sent home to prepare for the acceptance of Texas as an independent state, with the Rio Grande set as the boundary between the two.

Most Mexicans refused to accept this treaty, and fighting between Mexico and the Republic of Texas escalated. It did not take long for Americans to develop a negative attitude toward Mexicans and their government. In 1845 Texas was annexed by the United States, and hostilities soared. Texas claimed and Mexico reclaimed the border of the Rio Grande (then called the Río Bravo del Norte). On April 25, 1846, as troops began to battle over ownership of the soil, the Mexican War officially began. When it ended two years later, the United States had acquired the northern half of Mexico, now known as California, Nevada, Arizona, New Mexico, and Utah, and 13,780 Americans and approximately 25,000 Mexicans had lost their lives.

The duties of his new office required that Fillmore live in the state capital. He and Abigail, who still had spells of weakness, set up house in Albany. His son, Powers, was studying law at Harvard. Mary Abigail was in a finishing school in Massachusetts.

Fillmore took his new post quite seriously. As comptroller he was able to arrange for financing the enlargement of the New York State canals that were so important to commerce. He rallied support to reverse the "Stop and Tax" law, which stopped all canal construction except for necessary repairs. Most notably, he outlined a reform of the state banking code, which would prove so successful that the federal government would base the National Banking Act on it sixteen years later. These were remarkable accomplishments considering that Fillmore only served as comptroller for one year.

SAVING THE PARTY

In the spring of 1848 the Whig Party was in disarray. The backing of northern Whigs for their next presidential candidate was split

BEYOND POLITICS

In addition to his political career, Fillmore also got involved in supporting public education. He served as the first chancellor of the newly opened University at Buffalo in 1846. After he became president following President Taylor's death, he stayed on as part-time chancellor. Even today, Fillmore's name can be found all over the campus. It is even on the official stationery. The Millard Fillmore College is the university's night school, and one of the main academic halls is the Millard Fillmore Academic Center.

As New York State comptroller, Fillmore supported the expansion of the New York State canal system.

among Massachusetts senator Daniel Webster, General Winfield Scott, and former secretary of state Henry Clay, each of them, to differing degrees, advocates of the antislavery cause. Southern Whigs unanimously supported General Zachary Taylor, a hero of the Mexican War. Although Taylor was a Louisiana slaveholder, he had considerable support among northern Whigs, particularly in Democratic strongholds such as New York City, where it was thought that foreign-born Democrats might be persuaded to abandon their party's ticket to vote for him. Those westerners who favored the extension of slavery to the new territories acquired in the Mexican War also backed Taylor.

At the convention northern Whigs could not agree on a candidate, and Taylor was nominated on the fourth vote. Chaos followed. Charles Allen of Massachusetts leaped onto a table and shouted that "the free states will not submit! The party, by this nomination, is dissolved!"

His declaration might have come true had not John A. Collier, a Henry Clay backer, captured the podium. He gave an eloquent speech in which he made a peace offering in the form of a vice presidential nomination that would mollify his fellow northerners without offending southern Whigs. The man he would suggest was by no means an abolitionist but rather was a moderate on the question of slavery. Collier paused until the hall fell silent. Then he spoke the name they had been waiting to hear: Millard Fillmore!

A Betrayal Foiled

Fillmore was nominated on the second vote. Nevertheless, southern Whigs did not accept his being on the ticket. It made them vulnerable to charges from southern Democrats that an antislavery candidate was their choice for vice president. Nor were they sure themselves where Fillmore stood on the issue.

Fillmore reassured them, stating his view that the national government should have nothing to do with slavery. "By the constitution of the United States," he said, "the whole power over that question was vested in the several states where the institution was tolerated. If they regarded it as a blessing, they had a constitutional right to enjoy it." He concluded that he "did not conceive that Congress had any power over it, or was in any way responsible for its continuance over the several states where it existed."

An 1848 presidential campaign poster for Whig candidates Zachary Taylor and Millard Fillmore.

Southerners, however, were not the only ones threatening the Taylor-Fillmore ticket. Thurlow Weed, urged on by the zealous antislavery newspaper publisher Horace Greeley, was considering abandoning the party and using his power to have New York Whigs select a panel of unpledged presidential electors who could make up a swing vote in a close election and perhaps even force a compromise on the president of the nation. (A similar outcome had occurred in the election of 1824, in which Andrew Jackson had received the most votes of any of the four candidates, but since it was not a majority of the votes, the electors were able to choose John Quincy Adams as president.) If the plot succeeded, Weed would in effect be a national kingmaker.

Fillmore confronted Weed. It was a stormy meeting, but as a result, the mass meeting Weed had organized to announce his abandonment of the Taylor-Fillmore ticket was turned into a forum to support it. Fillmore and Weed addressed a letter to Taylor, assuring him of the Weed faction's backing.

Fillmore and Taylor did receive that backing on election day. Taylor and Fillmore were elected. Millard Fillmore was the vice president of the United States. He now held the most influential post of any New York Whig in the new administration, or so he believed. Thurlow Weed, however, saw matters differently.

PERFIDY AND PATRONAGE

*T*he Whig ticket on which Taylor and Fillmore were elected president and vice president also elected William Henry Seward as a senator from New York. Seward was a former New York State governor. He had been a leader of the Anti-Masonic Party before becoming a Whig. Significantly, Seward owed much of his political success to Thurlow Weed and worked hand-in-glove with him.

President Taylor had been elected as a Whig, but as a slaveholder, his support from the northern Whig leadership, which was mostly antislavery, was very shaky. At the same time the question of whether slavery was to be permitted in the territories acquired under the terms of the **Treaty of Guadalupe Hidalgo**, which ended the Mexican War in February 1848, was of great concern to southern Whigs. They looked to Taylor to side with them on the issue. Victory in the Mexican War had resulted in the United States acquiring an area of 1.2 million square miles, including

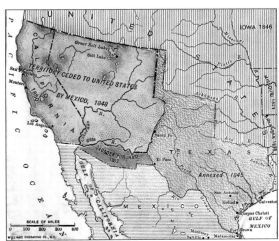

A map illustrates the territory ceded by Mexico to the United States after the victory in the Mexican War.

the future states of California, New Mexico, and Arizona, as well as major portions of Utah, Nevada, and Colorado. When added to the annexation of Texas in 1845, the land area of the United States had increased by 66 percent. Would these new territories allow slavery? This was the major issue during Taylor's presidency.

THE CALIFORNIA PLOT

A plan was devised by Taylor and his advisors that would pacify antislavery Whigs without causing southern slaveholders to blame the president. Thomas Butler King, a Taylor loyalist, was sent with several army officers to California, a territory known to be heavily antislavery. King met with powerful California Whig politicians and persuaded them to hold a convention to draft a constitution barring slavery and to create a new state. This was technically illegal. However, Taylor's plan was to have the military officers with King turn over their authority as military governors to the new "state." Two senators selected by the convention would then proceed to Washington and present their credentials to be seated in the U.S. Senate. Anticipating opposition to the legality of this maneuver, Taylor acted in advance of the California senators' arrival. He lined up support for having them seated, a necessary first step in securing recognition of California's statehood.

One of the first senators Taylor approached for support was Seward. He was a leader of the Senate's northern Whigs, but even more important to Taylor was Seward's well-known connection to Thurlow Weed. The Whig power broker's cooperation was key to the behind-the-scenes wheeling and dealing necessary to overcome any northern senators' resistance to the rule-bending California plot. Weed and Seward would have certain demands in return, of course, but Taylor was prepared to accommodate them.

In accommodating them, Taylor would be pulling the political rug out from under the feet of Vice President Millard Fillmore. An important part of political power for officeholders like Fillmore was the ability to dispense **patronage**. This meant being able to influence the appointment of government officials—judges, postmasters, land office managers, park supervisors, harbor captains. Patronage also involved awarding government contracts for highway construction, port facilities, military installations, and bridge and tunnel maintenance. As vice president and the highest-ranking New Yorker in the national administration, Fillmore naturally assumed that he would control patronage in New York State. After all, hadn't he interceded with Thurlow Weed to carry the state for President Taylor? But he hadn't counted on President Taylor recognizing that Weed's power was much more important to him than any vice president's could be.

CUT OUT OF THE LOOP

Fillmore behaved in the spirit of cooperation. He approached Seward to consult with him about patronage appointments. The New York senator, citing a heavy workload, asked for time to consider. "I have stipulated," Seward wrote Weed, "for time and inaction concerning marshals, postmasters, district-attorneys, and there I leave these matters."

When they finally did meet, Fillmore and Seward, who was acting for Weed, could not agree on whom to recommend for various posts. At this point Weed went to Washington and met with President Taylor. He convinced Taylor that the struggle between Fillmore and Seward was strictly personal. He suggested that Taylor end it by putting all patronage decisions in the hands of New York Governor Hamilton Fish, and Taylor agreed. Governor Fish was, of course, completely controlled by Boss Weed.

A series of recommendations by Fillmore for patronage posts in New York was denied by the president. In each case the appointment went to a candidate suggested by Governor Fish and favored by Weed. At the same time, Weed conducted a campaign throughout several New York counties to bad-mouth Fillmore and ensure that candidates he favored in the off-year elections were replaced by Weed favorites. Weed unleashed a press campaign criticizing Fillmore and pointing out that a vice president had no real clout in New York State politics.

As a result Fillmore's political allies deserted him, his influence sank to a low point, and his approval rating with the general public nosedived, along with his standing in the Whig Party. Fillmore's political organization in New York was in shambles, and he had virtually no access to President Taylor when it came to patronage or to influencing policies. Vice President Millard Fillmore was isolated politically. He was also leading a solitary life; Abigail's still-undiagnosed condition was growing worse, and she had been too weak to accompany him to Washington.

President Taylor's Proposal

As vice president, Fillmore presided over the Senate. For the most part this position was powerless, for he could not vote except in the case of ties. That exception, however, might possibly provide Fillmore with the means to push through a compromise on the issue of slavery and end a standoff that could lead the South to secede and break the Union in two. The measure to be voted on would become known as the Compromise of 1850.

It began with a proposal to Congress by President Taylor that California and New Mexico be admitted to the Union and allowed to decide for themselves if they would be free or slave states. Since California had already voted against slavery and New Mexico was likely to do the same, Congress, which was controlled by Democrats—the majority of whom were proslavery southerners—would never approve Taylor's proposal. They were afraid that it would tip the balance between free and slave states in favor of the North.

The South reacted. Merchants throughout the North were deluged with letters from southern customers canceling orders because of the "agitation of the great national questions in Washington." Articles began appearing in northern newspapers pointing out how the economy would crash if the South should be forced to secede by abolitionist laws passed in Washington. Northern business interests responded. Northern senators were pressured not to pass any legislation that might further alienate the South. By mid-February 1850, six southern states had appointed delegates to a convention in Nashville at which **secession** would be discussed.

THE FUGITIVE SLAVE ACT

Henry S. Foote, a Democratic senator from Mississippi, proposed a plan more favorable to the South than the president's proposal. In it, all of the issues related to secession and slavery would be delegated to a thirteen-member committee that would organize the proposals into an official legislative plan. Although Foote would stand by his plan over the following months, northerners would not accept it. On January 29, 1850, two weeks after Senator Foote presented his plan, seventy-three-year-old senator

Henry Clay of Kentucky introduced "an amiable arrangement of all questions in controversy between the free and slave states growing out of the subject of slavery." His proposal was that California be admitted as a free state, and that New Mexico be divided into two territories that would, after they became states, decide whether to allow slavery within each of their borders. He also proposed that the slave trade be outlawed in Washington, D.C., and that a much stronger Fugitive Slave Act be passed and enforced to replace the ineffective one that was then on the books. The **Fugitive Slave Acts of 1793** provided that any slave who escaped to another state or into federal territory would be seized and returned to his or her owner. The **Fugitive Slave Act of 1850,** supported by Senator Clay, imposed an additional penalty on any individual who helped a slave escape.

Henry Clay proposes his California Compromise to the Senate in 1850.

The idea of a new, strong fugitive slave act immediately aroused opposition from anti-slavery Whigs. Senator Seward called it "a pact with the devil" and urged that northern states secede from the Union if it were ever enforced. It had been intended to mollify southerners, but many southerners opposed Clay's compromise because they didn't believe the North would ever cooperate in enforcing the Fugitive Slave Act.

The debate raged on in the Senate. Senator Foote argued heatedly with fellow Democratic senator Thomas Hart Benton of Missouri. Presiding over the Senate, Vice President Fillmore

A runaway slave is hunted down under the rules of the Fugitive Slave Acts.

repeatedly banged his gavel to demand order, to no avail. Finally, Senator Foote, an undersized bald man with a hot temper, pulled out a pistol and threatened Benton. With senators scrambling to get out of the way, Fillmore calmly ordered that the senator be disarmed. Towering over the proceedings, the vice president stood erect, unafraid, and spoke authoritatively until order was restored.

An Uncast Vote

As spring passed into summer, pressure in the Senate increased to force a vote on a revised version of the Clay proposal. President

KIDNAPPERS AND WATCHMEN

The Fugitive Slave Act of 1850 placed pressure on authorities and slaves. Any federal marshal or other official who failed to arrest an alleged runaway could be fined $1,000. It became the duty of the authorities to arrest anyone even suspected of running away, often with little or no evidence at all. Those arrested were not allowed a jury trial, nor were they given the chance to testify on their own behalf. The restrictions did not stop there, however. Under this law anyone who helped a runaway was subject to six months in prison and another $1,000 fine. To make arresting a slave even more tempting, officers were paid a bonus for each runaway they brought in.

A poster (right) issued in April 1851 warned the African Americans of Boston that policemen would be acting as slave catchers.

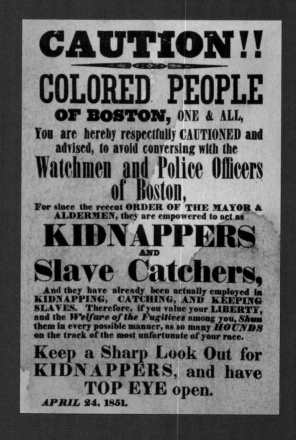

CAUTION!!

COLORED PEOPLE
OF BOSTON, ONE & ALL,
You are hereby respectfully CAUTIONED and advised, to avoid conversing with the
Watchmen and Police Officers of Boston,
For since the recent ORDER OF THE MAYOR & ALDERMEN, they are empowered to act as
KIDNAPPERS
AND
Slave Catchers,
And they have already been actually employed in KIDNAPPING, CATCHING, AND KEEPING SLAVES. Therefore, if you value your LIBERTY, and the Welfare of the Fugitives among you, Shun them in every possible manner, as so many HOUNDS on the track of the most unfortunate of your race.
Keep a Sharp Look Out for KIDNAPPERS, and have TOP EYE open.
APRIL 24, 1851.

Taylor, stubbornly insisting on his own bill, was vehemently opposed to passing Clay's. Taylor's bill stood no chance of passing, however, as long as Clay's proposal was more acceptable to northern senators who had been pressured by business interests and even by some southerners. It became increasingly obvious that the vote on Clay's bill would be an extremely close one and that it might well be a tie that could only be broken by the vice president. Fillmore was besieged with queries from politicians and journalists asking how he would vote, but he refused to say. When the vote became imminent, however, he went to the White House and revealed his intentions to President Taylor. He told the president that if he should feel it his duty to vote for the bill "as I might, I wished him to understand that it was not out of any hostility to him or his Administration, but the vote would be given because I deemed it for the best interests of the country."

It was an odd reversal of roles. Taylor, the slave owner from Louisiana, was trying to force the Senate to accept a bill that would tip the balance of power in favor of the antislavery North. Fillmore, the northern Whig who said privately that he deplored slavery, was intending to vote for a bill that would force his fellow New Yorkers to return fugitive slaves to their southern owners.

However, Fillmore never had to cast that deciding vote. On the Fourth of July President Taylor stood for hours in the hot sun, listening to patriotic speeches with his head uncovered. The next day he fell sick. Then, on July 9, 1850, President Zachary Taylor died of a sudden illness that his doctors called cholera morbus. Millard Fillmore was sworn in as the thirteenth president of the United States.

PRESIDENT OR OPPRESSOR?

Five

*T*he swearing in of Millard Fillmore as president of the United States took place on July 10, 1850. Neither Abigail Fillmore nor the Fillmore children were present for his inauguration. They had set out from Buffalo as soon as they heard of the death of President Taylor, but had not been able to get to Washington in time for the ceremony.

Fillmore served as president until March 4, 1853—a little more than two and a half years. During his time in office he faced many issues and had some accomplishments and some failures. One question, however, dominated his administration and characterized it for the history books. This was his signing and enforcement of the Fugitive Slave Act of 1850.

The original Fugitive Slave Acts stated that any slave who escaped to another state or into federal territories would be captured and returned to his or her owner. In 1850 this was expanded so that any individual who assisted in a slave's escape would be penalized with either a fine or a prison sentence. This meant that a newly created group of federal commissioners was instructed to chase runaway slaves into any state and bring them back. They would get $10 for each runaway, but only $5 if the returned slave was let go by his or her owner. There was no time limit, either; even slaves who had been free for years could be caught and returned. These slaves were not allowed to have any kind of trial.

This act was one of the five separate measures of the revised omnibus compromise bill originally proposed by Senator Clay. The **omnibus bill** was debated hotly in the Senate during the days immediately following President Fillmore's inauguration. Fillmore let it be known that he would sign the omnibus bill if the Senate passed it, and that if it failed to pass, he would sign into law any parts of the bill the Senate submitted to him, providing they were constitutional.

When the omnibus bill failed to pass in the Senate, the individual sections were revised, sent to the president, and immediately signed by him. The last to reach his desk was the Fugitive Slave Act. He told associates that signing it would draw down on his head "vials of wrath" from

A day after the sudden death of President Zachary Taylor, Millard Fillmore wrote to Congress, "I have to perform the melancholy duty of announcing to you that it has pleased Almighty God to remove from this life Zachary Taylor. . . . I propose . . . to take the oath prescribed by the Constitution."

abolitionists. Nevertheless, after consulting with his attorney general, John J. Crittenden—a southern Whig—Fillmore signed the Fugitive Slave Act into law. He said that the U.S. Constitution required the recapture of fugitive slaves—who were, after all, the lawful property of their owners—and that as president, he was sworn to uphold the Constitution.

Union or Equality

Attorney General Crittenden was one of the first people appointed by the new president. The Taylor presidential cabinet, which had supported Taylor's opposition to the Clay omnibus compromise bill, had all offered their resignations to Fillmore on the eve of his inauguration. Aware of their role in curtailing his influence in the Taylor administration, Fillmore accepted their resignations. He then formed his own cabinet, with Crittenden as attorney general, Daniel Webster as secretary of state, and his former law partner, Nathan K. Hall, as postmaster general—the main patronage-dispensing post in the cabinet. He tried to balance his cabinet with southerners and northerners, but demanded of both that they value the Union above both sectionalism and their position on slavery. The preservation of the Union and the enforcement of the law would be the main principles of the Fillmore administration, and the settlement of the slavery question would be shelved.

Slavery, however, was still very much the primary issue throughout the country. In particular, there was the obligation the Fugitive Slave Act placed on northerners to cooperate in returning escaped slaves to their owners or face penalties. When the president signed the measure, the response from some northern abolitionists was threats of physical violence against him, along with anti-Fillmore signs bearing skulls and crossbones. Southerners who favored secession from the Union predicted that northerners would not cooperate with the law, no matter what the penalties were. Fillmore, who viewed compliance with the law as necessary to the preservation of the Union, was determined that the Fugitive Slave Act should not be undermined.

President Fillmore was not, perhaps, considering the determination of the slaves to be free. Some runaways endured incredible hardships—wading through alligator-infested swamps, risking snakebites in caves used as hideouts, clinging to the bottoms of speeding freight cars, running from bloodhounds and the bullets of slave catchers. They faced brutal whippings and brandings with hot irons to create identifying marks if they were captured. They risked everything to get out of the slaveholding South to what they regarded as the safety of the North. Some were lucky and found refuge or were passed along by the Underground Railroad to Canada. Some were recaptured under the

In their quest for freedom, slaves sometimes traveled the Underground Railroad and endured harsh conditions.

terms of the Fugitive Slave Act. All were striving for an ideal every bit as important to them as the Union was to President Fillmore. The ideal was freedom.

That ideal was so important to former slaves like Harriet Tubman, Elijah Anderson, and John Mason that they repeatedly returned to the South to lead groups of slaves to the North. One slave, Henry "Box" Brown, literally mailed himself to freedom. He encased himself in a box three feet long and two feet deep and was carried by Adams Express for the twenty-six hours it took to travel from Richmond, Virginia, to Philadelphia. Some slaves were forced to leave their children behind when they fled. Many did not run away because they could not bear to do that. Either way, the enslaved Africans yearned for freedom.

The Christiana Riot

Antislavery sentiment ran high in the North, and abolitionist leaders were determined to put Fillmore's decision to enforce the Fugitive Slave Act to the test. Much of their opposition was religiously based. They claimed that there was a higher law than any Fugitive Slave Act. God's law, they said, decreed that all men were free. More and more they agreed with antislavery advocates such as William Lloyd Garrison and Henry David Thoreau that **civil disobedience** was justified in the form of resisting the return of runaway slaves to their owners.

The inevitable confrontation occurred on September 11, 1851, in the Quaker community of Christiana, Pennsylvania. Three deputy marshals, a Maryland slave owner, and several of his relatives arrived in the town—a known haven for fugitive slaves— seeking two runaway slaves. When they located the runaways, they found them protected by two-dozen armed black men. Two white Quakers, believers in nonviolence, told the slave catchers that their lives were at risk and tried to persuade them to leave Christiana. The slave owner answered, "I will have my property, or I'll eat my breakfast in hell."

Shots were fired on both sides. When the smoke cleared, the slave owner was dead and his son seriously wounded. Two other whites and two blacks were also wounded. The leaders of the resistance and the two slaves who had been sought for recapture fled, making their way to Canada via the Underground Railroad.

News of the **Christiana Riot**, as it was called by newspapers in the North and South, aroused both proslavery and antislavery advocates. A Pennsylvania newspaper titled the story about it "Civil War—The First Blow Struck." Southerners threatened to leave the Union "unless the Christiana rioters are hung." Pressure grew on President Fillmore to take action. The action he took was predetermined by his decision to enforce the Fugitive Slave Act. He called out the Marines.

THE TREASON TRIALS

Backed by the Marines, federal marshals in the Christiana area arrested thirty-six African Americans, along with six whites. Citing the U.S. extradition treaty with Canada, President Fillmore's representatives demanded the return of three Christiana fugitives who had fled to Ontario. The Canadian government refused to return the men. The Fillmore administration then charged the people that the Marines had rounded up with treason, rather than with just breaking the law.

Throughout the North the decision to charge the rioters with treason was ridiculed. One abolitionist pointed out that "these Treason Trials have been a great windfall" for the antislavery movement, as northern outrage fueled the antislavery cause. President Fillmore's popularity plummeted even further. Cartoons and editorials printed in northern newspapers were vicious in their mockery of him.

The first defendant in the treason trials was a Quaker. The jury quickly acquitted him. The storm of protest and ridicule over the treason charges forced the Fillmore administration to rethink its position. The government halted the prosecution of the rioters for treason and declined to press charges against them under the Fugitive Slave Act or for any other reason. The defendants were freed.

THE FAILED POLICY

However, it was too late for Fillmore to recapture his popularity in the North, and in the South his decision to release the defendants was met with outrage. It was regarded as proof that the federal government—no matter what it said or what laws it passed—would not support southern property rights where escaped slaves were concerned. The governor of South Carolina announced that "there is now not the slightest doubt but that . . . the state will secede."

Secession was the one thing President Fillmore was determined to prevent. The preservation of the Union was still his main goal. To do this, he stepped up the use of federal troops to enforce the Fugitive Slave Act. The actions of these troops in places like Boston, Syracuse, New York, and Philadelphia further infuriated northerners. At the same time the failure of the Act to stop the increasing number of successful flights by fugitive slaves increased southern sentiment for secession.

According to his detractors on both sides of the **Mason-Dixon Line,** President Fillmore's enforcement of the Fugitive Slave Act was a disaster. To his few supporters, the president was achieving his goal; he was preserving the Union. But in fact, in the early 1850s, a decade before the Civil War, it was cotton that was holding the Union together. The South was producing the largest cotton crops in many years, and the price of cotton was soaring throughout the United States as well as on the world market. The plantation owners who pretty much controlled southern politics did not, at that point in time, favor secession. It would have severely cut into their profits.

Southern plantation owners, wealthy from their bountiful cotton crops, did not favor secession from the Union during the early 1850s.

American naval officer Commodore Matthew Perry opened trade between Japan and the United States.

COMMODORE PERRY'S JAPANESE EXPEDITION

The controversy over slavery obscured other events and accomplishments of the Fillmore presidency. Millard Fillmore was a strong advocate of advancing the nation's welfare by promoting shipping and trade exports and developing foreign markets. His greatest success in this area was the assignment of Commodore Matthew Perry to establish trade relations with Japan.

In 1853 Japan was a nation that had chosen to isolate itself, with only one port, Nagasaki, open to foreign commerce. That one port was receiving only Dutch ships at that time. The nineteenth-century Japanese were suspicious of foreigners in general, and when shipwrecked American sailors washed up on Japanese soil, they were taken prisoner and treated badly. Japanese policy was to regard foreign trade as an invasion of Japanese culture.

When Commodore Perry, with introductory letters from President Fillmore, sailed into Edo Bay, Japanese officials ordered him to proceed to Nagasaki. He refused, making a counteroffer instead that allowed the Japanese to inspect his small fleet's state-of-the-art cannons. They accepted and were so impressed that Perry was allowed to meet with representatives of the emperor.

After many such meetings Perry was able to negotiate the

Japanese watch the first U.S. naval ships enter Edo Bay in July 1853.

Treaty of Peace and Amity, which opened up Japanese ports to American shipping. The treaty also guaranteed the safety of American sailors who were forced to land in Japan. Over the years it not only proved to be a boon to American trade but also brought Japan into the community of world nations where, in the future, it would play a significant role.

ACCOMPLISHMENTS AND FAILURES

President Fillmore was the driving force in the opening of Japan to foreign markets. He also played an important part in developing the railroads that would eventually crisscross the United States. When he was a congressman he campaigned successfully for federal land grants for railroads. As president he championed the cause of building a transcontinental railroad, a project that would be completed after his presidency ended.

There were failures as well. In order to facilitate American trade in the Pacific, he worked to arrange a treaty that would allow a canal joining the Atlantic and Pacific oceans to be built in Nicaragua. This would allow boats to travel between the two oceans without having to sail all the way around South America. The main trade rival of the United States was England. Acting in collusion with local Nicaraguan leaders, the British blocked the building of the canal. Only decades later would the canal be built through Panama instead of Nicaragua.

An attempt by Fillmore to build a railroad line across the Isthmus of Tehuantepec in Mexico to speed up shipping in the Pacific also failed. When he appointed the Mormon church leader Brigham Young to be the territorial governor of Utah, his judgment was questioned, and he suffered great embarrassment, for Young openly promoted—and indulged in—polygamy (the practice of having several wives). James Buchanan, who assumed the presidency two terms after Fillmore, had to send federal troops to remove Young from his position.

Sadly, Fillmore was not a president who would be remembered for his accomplishments. Instead, history would remember him as the president who signed the Fugitive Slave Act into law and enforced it with military might.

President Fillmore supported the transcontinental railroad that would, upon completion, open trade from coast to coast.

Bringing In the Books

Both Abigail and Millard Fillmore shared a similar passion—books. During their childhoods each of them had turned to the lessons and entertainment that could be found between the covers of a book. Abigail's father died when she was young but left his family a sizable collection of books, which she used to help further her education. Millard, on the other hand, turned to the local library for his education. "I went to school some," he wrote, "during the winters of 1816 and 1817, and worked on the farm during the spring. I had thus far had no access to books, beyond the schoolbooks which I had; as my father's library consisted only of a Bible, hymn-book and almanac, and sometimes a little weekly paper from Auburn; but in 1817 or 1818 a small circulating library was established in the town, and I managed to get a share, which cost me two dollars. Then, for the first time, I began to read miscellaneous works."

During their marriage the Fillmores developed an impressive library in their home in New York. When they moved into the White House, they were shocked to find out that not only did it not have a library, it didn't have any books. It didn't even have a Bible or a dictionary. They immediately decided to change that.

After being granted permission by Congress to purchase books, Abigail went to work. She moved a piano and harp into the White House's oval room on the second floor. She ordered mahogany bookcases capable of holding several hundred books to be constructed around the oddly shaped room. She turned to the world's most respected writers to fill the shelves, including Shakespeare, Dickens, and Thackeray. She also purchased a mixture of travel books, poetry, biographies, religious works, and fictional novels. In addition, she hosted a number of influential writers at the White House. The pleasant room became the gathering place for family and visitors alike. According to the author Laura Carter Holloway in her book *The Ladies of the White House* (1883), "Here Mrs. Fillmore surrounded herself with her own little home comforts: here her daughter had her own piano, harp and guitar and here Mrs. Fillmore received the informal visits of the friends she loved, and for her the real pleasures and enjoyments of the White House were in this room."

THE FINAL YEARS

*I*n November 1850, only four months after he became president, Millard Fillmore addressed the question of his reelection in a letter to a friend. "I believe I am holding the last office that I shall ever hold," he wrote, adding that he had "no desire to prolong it one minute beyond the constitutional time." By the time of the Whig presidential convention in June of 1852, however, Fillmore had changed his mind and actively sought reelection.

The convention was held in Baltimore in sweltering heat that was unrelieved by air-conditioning or electric fans, neither of which had been invented yet. Nomination for president required 147 votes. On the first vote President Fillmore received 133 votes. Of these, 114 were cast by delegates from the South. General Winfield Scott, a Mexican War hero backed by Thurlow Weed and Senator William Seward, received 131 votes. The remaining twenty-nine votes went to Daniel Webster of Massachusetts.

After six rounds of voting, there was only a shift of one or two votes, and the deadlock continued. The convention adjourned for the day. That evening Whig Party leaders stayed up late trying to arrange a compromise that would end the standoff. They failed. By 2 p.m. the next day delegates had voted thirty-one times, and the situation remained unchanged. The assembly adjourned for two hours. When the delegates reconvened, the number of votes taken rose to forty-six, and the sweltering convention attendees decided to adjourn until the following Monday.

Early Monday morning Daniel Webster sent a note to President Fillmore saying that he was going to release the delegates who supported him in order to "have an end put to the pending controversy." He predicted that Fillmore "will be nominated before 1 o'clock." However, when two southern delegates switched their votes from Fillmore to Scott on the forty-eighth vote, the Webster delegates also began switching to Scott, rather than to President Fillmore. As the voting continued, Scott received more and more support from the Webster delegates. Finally, on the fifty-third vote, General Winfield Scott was nominated as the Whig candidate for president of the United States. In the general election that followed, he was defeated by Democrat Franklin Pierce.

TRAGEDY STRIKES

The inauguration day of March 4, 1853, was marked by tragedy for both the new president and Millard Fillmore. Franklin Pierce's son was killed in a railroad accident while on his way to the ceremony in Washington. Although she had been ill for some time, Abigail Fillmore insisted on accompanying her husband to the event that would mark the end of his presidency. It was a chill, damp day, and Abigail's lips were pinched and blue. She kept moving her feet in the slush of melting snow to keep them warm. By the end of the ceremony she was shivering and her teeth were chattering. The next day she had a severe cold and was running a high fever. It soon developed into pneumonia. After three weeks of illness, on March 30, Abigail Fillmore died.

Even through her illness the quiet and unassuming Abigail had provided key support for her husband's career. He often discussed his decisions with her before reaching or modifying them. She had a calming effect and often was a restraining influence on him. Devastated, Fillmore accompanied his wife's body back to Buffalo, where Abigail was buried.

In Buffalo he set up house with his twenty-one-year-old daughter, Mary Abigail. The first year of his retirement was marked by a bitterness that was not helped by the absence of his beloved wife. Although he had a modest income from investments he made during his years as a successful lawyer, Fillmore worried about money. He considered it "a national disgrace" that presidents "should be cast adrift" financially once they were out of office.

By the spring of 1854 Fillmore rallied and became active in politics again. He traveled around the country, addressing meetings of Whigs. Then, without warning, tragedy struck again. At the end of July, Mary Abigail, who had tried so hard to replace her mother in Fillmore's life, was taken ill. Within a few hours of the first signs of her illness, she died of cholera.

THE KNOW-NOTHING PARTY

The twice-bereaved Fillmore now fought loneliness with renewed political activity. In January 1855 he wrote a letter deploring the "corrupting influence" of the competition for immigrant votes among politicians. The letter was addressed to Isaac Newton Blackford, a leader of the so-called **Know-Nothing Party**.

Officially named the **American Party**, the Know-Nothings were an offshoot of the anti-immigrant, nativist movement of the previous decade. The organization had begun as a secret society, called the **Order of the Star-Spangled Banner**, in New York City in 1849. Its members were American-born Protestants. Its nickname came from the policy of members answering questions about the American Party's platform with the words "I know nothing."

Prejudice against German, Irish, and other immigrants, particularly Catholics, had reached its peak in the United States by the mid-1850s. Many of these immigrants, barred from all but the most menial jobs, were crowded into large cities. There the pressure of large numbers of poor people and the lack of adequate sewers and garbage collection services turned these areas into filthy, disease-ridden slums. The politicians running the large cities had been reluctant to authorize payment for such social services. This began to change when the immigrants organized, became citizens, and

A Know-Nothing cartoon supports the accusation that Irish and German immigrants were stealing American elections and influencing big-city politics.

used the power of their votes to push through laws to alleviate their terrible living conditions. The votes of the foreign-born were fast becoming the deciding political factor in elections in New York, Buffalo, Boston, Chicago, and other large cities.

When Millard Fillmore wrote of the "corrupting influence" of the immigrants, the ex-president was in agreement with the policies of the Know-Nothings. These called for excluding Catholics and foreigners from public office. Know-Nothings campaigned for a law that would keep the foreign-born from applying for U.S. citizenship for a period of twenty-one years after their date of arrival in the country. They demanded strict quotas to restrict future immigration. They advocated laws barring the foreign-born from holding office at every level of city, state, and federal government. They believed that only Protestant children should be admitted to public schools and demanded that a Protestant version of the Bible be read daily in all of the nation's classrooms. Bigotry toward all but Anglo-Saxon white Protestants filled their party literature and was repeated in speeches delivered by Know-Nothing leaders.

The Oath and the Prediction

By the midterm elections of 1854, Know-Nothing membership had risen at a phenomenal rate. General stores were selling Know-Nothing Candy, Know-Nothing Tea, and Know-Nothing Toothpicks. A clipper ship was christened *Know-Nothing* in a New York City launch. The Know-Nothings had become a major force in American politics. In the elections Know-Nothings carried Massachusetts and Delaware. Through an alliance with the Whigs, they also carried Pennsylvania. They sent seventeen congressmen to Washington. They showed great strength in the South, and elected officials in Texas. In the rest of the West, however, they had weak support.

The surprise of the election was the Know-Nothing vote in New York State. The candidate for governor, Daniel Ullman, didn't win, but he got 122,000 votes, at that time a huge number for a minor-party candidate. Fillmore was impressed. He urged his political allies to join the Know-Nothing movement. "Give it a proper direction," he urged them, and make it "a truly national party."

By the mid-1850s, the Know-Nothing Party had many members. The party was promoted on many daily items, such as bars of soap.

Early in 1855, following his New Year's Day letter to Isaac Newton Blackford, the ex-president was clandestinely inducted into the Order of the Star-Spangled Banner. The secret rites were administered in the library of his home. After Fillmore had sworn an oath of allegiance, Charles McComber, who had presided over the initiation, said, "Mr. Fillmore, you have taken this step which will certainly land you in the presidential chair at Washington." "Charles," Millard Fillmore responded, "I trust so."

THE KANSAS-NEBRASKA ACT

During the following year Fillmore toured Europe. He was still out of the country in June of 1856 when the national convention of the American Party was held. With only a few dissenting votes, Fillmore was chosen as the Know-Nothing candidate for president.

He would be running against General John Charles Frémont, the choice of the newly formed Republican Party, which was made up of mostly antislavery former Whigs, and the Democrat James Buchanan of Pennsylvania. Many of those Whigs who had not become Republicans supported Fillmore and the Know-Nothings. When Fillmore returned from abroad, the American Party organized a welcome for his ship that included a fifty-gun salute and a colorful display of rockets.

The main issue of the 1856 presidential race was the passage, two years earlier, of the **Kansas-Nebraska Act.** The act had repealed the Missouri Compromise of 1820, which forbade slavery in any U.S. territories north of latitude 36° 30'. It called for a vote by the residents of Kansas and Nebraska to decide whether each should be a slave or free state. Before the first election could be held, proslavery and antislavery supporters had rushed to Kansas to affect the outcome. Proslavery settlers won the election, but antislavery Kansans claimed that there had been fraud and refused to accept the results. When a second election was held, the proslavery citizens refused to vote in it. The result was that Kansas had two opposing legislatures. To complicate matters, there was disagreement between the two groups over the route to be taken by the proposed transcontinental railroad. Questions were also raised as to whether it would be built with slave or free labor once it crossed the Kansas border.

An 1856 "Nothing but my Country" campaign ribbon.

General Frémont and the Republican Party were against allowing slavery in Kansas. The Democrats were from the party of the proslavery South, and their candidate, James Buchanan, although a northerner, supported their cause. Fillmore, pointing to the bloodshed in Kansas, attacked the politicians who passed the Kansas-Nebraska bill as having "recklessly and wantonly" done so "to aid in personal advancement." Lashing out at Frémont, he warned that "our Southern brethren" would not "submit to be governed by such a Chief Magistrate."

Fillmore's attacks played a large part in costing Frémont the election, but the votes those attacks cost the Democratic candidate tipped the election toward the Republicans, rather than the Know-Nothings. In the end, although Fillmore received an impressive 21 percent of the popular vote (much of it from southern supporters and former Whigs), James Buchanan was elected president. In the era following the election the American Party went into decline, and the Know-Nothings soon ceased to be a major factor in U.S. politics.

Millard Fillmore retired from politics during the period preceding the Civil War. He lived quietly in Buffalo, and in 1858 he remarried. His bride was Mrs. Caroline McIntosh, a wealthy widow. Regarded as a public-spirited citizen, Fillmore founded the Buffalo General Hospital and worked to promote public libraries and schools. In 1861, when the Civil War broke out, he organized a company of older men, the **Union Continentals**, to defend Buffalo in the event that it should be attacked by Confederate forces. At the same time he was a bitter critic of Abraham Lincoln and the Republican Party, blaming them for plunging the nation into the conflict that was splitting up the Union.

After the war Fillmore did not participate much in debate or public life. He was not ill, but his age slowed him down. At the age of seventy-four he had a stroke. His speech was affected, and other functions were impaired. A month later, on March 8, 1874, Millard Fillmore died.

A REAL CALL TO ARMS

When President Abraham Lincoln made a passionate call for 75,000 volunteers to fight the Civil War in 1861, people responded with enthusiasm. Volunteers appeared from everywhere, lining up to dedicate their time and effort to support their country. Although history is not sure who originally came up with the idea for "a home and escort guard comprised of Buffalo's retired military officers," it is clear that the commander of these Union Continentals was former president Millard Fillmore, then sixty-one years old.

The Union Continentals wore uniforms consisting of a black frock and pants, as well as a buff-colored vest, white gloves, and a three-pointed hat. The troop consisted of former soldiers ranging from generals to captains, most of whom were at that point judges, lawyers, bankers, merchants, and real estate holders. They met twice a week to conduct drills and make plans. The men represented honor, respect, and dedication to their country.

For the duration of the war the Union Continentals performed a variety of duties, including attending funerals, walking in parades, saluting troops as they arrived and left for battle, and acting as a guard of honor when the assassinated Abraham Lincoln's remains lay in state in Buffalo, New York's St. James Hall.

Millard Fillmore, an "invisible man" among U.S. presidents, kept the United States from civil war for a decade.

TIMELINE

1800
Born on January 7 in Cayuga County, New York

1826
Marries Abigail Powers on February 25

1828
Elected to the New York State Legislature

1832
Elected to the U.S. Congress as an Anti-Masonic candidate

1836
Elected to Congress as a Whig

1841
Is chairman of the powerful House Ways and Means Committee

1844
Runs for governor of New York as a Whig and is defeated

1847
Elected comptroller of New York State; serves as chancellor of the University at Buffalo

1800

★ ★ ★ ★ ★ ★ ★ ★ ★ ★ ★ ★ ★ ★ ★ ★ ★ ★

1848
Elected vice president of the United States

1850
Becomes president after the death of President Zachary Taylor

1853
Presidential term ends; Abigail Fillmore dies

1855
Secretly sworn into the Order of the Star-Spangled Banner

1856
Chosen by the American Party as the Know-Nothing candidate for president; Democrat James Buchanan is elected president

1858
Marries Mrs. Caroline McIntosh

1874
Dies from complications from stroke

1900

Glossary

abolitionists individuals and organizations who were opposed to slavery

American Party official name of the Know-Nothing Party

American Republican Party organization formed by New York Whigs in 1842 to protect the interests of the native-born against inroads by the foreign-born

Anti-Masonic Party powerful third-party movement of the 1820s dedicated to outlawing the fraternal order of Masons and their practices

Christiana Riot Confrontation between slave catchers and anti-slavery advocates that took place in a Pennsylvania community on September 11, 1851; first test of the Fugitive Slave Act of 1850

civil disobedience nonviolent resistance to a law thought to be unjust

cotton Whigs southern plantation owners who favored high-tariff trade policies but opposed the antislavery policies of northern Whigs

free banking system in which banks operate as independent businesses, without interference or control by the government

Freemasons largest secret fraternal order in the world; a charitable and ethical organization that is sometimes a target of suspicion because of its confidential practices

free traders exporters who opposed high tariffs

Fugitive Slave Acts (1793) federal laws defining runaway slaves as property to be returned to their owners; signed into law by the president and slave owner George Washington

Fugitive Slave Act (1850) strengthened law signed by President Millard Fillmore, who enforced it with federal troops

heretic person who does not hold accepted beliefs or standards

Kansas-Nebraska Act (1854) controversial law that repealed the Missouri Compromise of 1820, which had limited the spread of slavery; it was a major issue in the election of 1856

Know-Nothing Party Anti-Catholic, anti-immigrant political party that gained power in the 1850s and unsuccessfully ran Millard Fillmore for president

Liberty Party first U.S. antislavery political organization

Manifest Destiny policy of extending U.S. territory from the Atlantic to the Pacific Ocean and annexing the land in between

Mason-Dixon Line the unofficial boundary between the North and South

Mexican War (April 1846–February 1848) conflict in which the United States acquired an additional 1.2 million square miles of territory, including California, New Mexico, and Arizona

nativism policy to restrict immigration and immigrants' rights

omnibus bill proposals for various laws lumped together in one package

Order of the Star-Spangled Banner secret society that formed the Know-Nothing Party

patronage awarding of contracts, government posts, and other favors to political party loyalists by those in power

protectionists manufacturers who, fearing that low-cost foreign goods would cut into their sales, favored high tariffs on imports

secession act of a state withdrawing from the Union

tariff tax on goods imported from outside the country

tenant farmer one who farms land owned by another and who is paid with a share of the crop or the profit it brings

Treaty of Guadalupe Hidalgo agreement that ended the Mexican War in February of 1848

Treaty of Peace and Amity trade agreement negotiated by Commodore Matthew Perry that opened up trade between the United States and Japan

Union Continentals militia made up of older men that was organized by Millard Fillmore during the Civil War to defend Buffalo

Whig Party major U.S. political party (1834–1854) that was formed by former Jeffersonian Republicans and members of the Anti-Masonic Party to oppose Andrew Jackson

FURTHER INFORMATION

BOOKS

Deem, James M. *Millard Fillmore*. Springfield, NJ: Enslow
Publishers, Inc., 2003.

Santella, Andrew. *Millard Fillmore: Profiles of the Presidents*.
Minneapolis: Compass Point Books, 2003.

Santow, Dan. *Millard Fillmore: America's 13th President*. Danbury,
CT: Children's Press, 2004.

Venezia, Mike. *Millard Fillmore: Thirteenth President 1850–1853*.
Danbury, CT: Children's Press, 2006.

WEB SITES

White House Biographies
www.whitehouse.gov/history/presidents/mf13.html
This is the official site of the White House Presidential Biographies.

Millard Fillmore
www.americanpresident.org/history/millardfillmore/
This site contains a brief biography of Millard Fillmore from the
American President Organization.

Millard Fillmore
www.millardfillmore.org/
This is a detailed biography from a site completely focused on Millard
Fillmore.

Presidents of the United States

www.historycentral.com/Bio/presidents/fillmore.html

This is a biography on Millard Fillmore from History Central.

History of Buffalo: Millard Fillmore

www.freenet.buffalo.edu/bah/h/mf/chron/

This site includes a biography of Millard Fillmore, as well as photographs and illustrations of his family, homes, and monuments.

BIBLIOGRAPHY

Asbury, Herbert. *The Gangs of New York*. New York: Thunder's Mouth Press, 1927, reissued 1998.

Barre, W. L. *Life and Public Services of Millard Fillmore*. New York: Burt Franklin, 1856, reprinted 1971.

McPherson, James M. *Battle Cry of Freedom: The Civil War Era*. New York: Oxford University Press, 1988.

Meltzer, Milton, and Walter Harding. *A Thoreau Profile*. Lincoln, MA: The Thoreau Society, 1962, reissued 1998.

Miller, William. *A New History of the United States*. New York: George Braziller, Inc., 1958.

Milner, Clyde A., Carol A. O'Connor, and Martha A. Sandweiss, ed. *The Oxford History of the American West*. New York: Oxford University Press, 1994.

Rayback, Robert J. *Millard Fillmore: Biography of a President*. Newtown, CT: American Political Biography Press, 1959.

Scarry, Robert J. *Millard Fillmore*. Jefferson, NC: McFarland & Company, Inc., Publishers, 2001.

Scott, John Anthony, and Robert Alan Scott. *John Brown of Harper's Ferry*. New York: Facts on File Publications, 1988.

White, Deborah Gray. *Let My People Go: African Americans 1804–1860*. New York: Oxford University Press, 1996.

INDEX

Pages in **boldface** are illustrations.

★ ★ ★ ★ ★ ★ ★ ★ ★ ★ ★ ★ ★ ★ ★ ★ ★

ABOUT THE AUTHOR

Ted Gottfried authored more than fifty books. During his long career he wrote both fiction and nonfiction, including award-winning biographies and histories for young adults. He was a native New Yorker, a resident of Manhattan who grew up in the Bronx and in Far Rockaway, Queens. He raised five children and two stepchildren. Gottfried was a member of the National Writer's Union and taught writing at New York University and Baruch College. He died in 2004.